SHAPES
ALL AROUND

A FIRST SHAPES BOOK

First published in this edition 2004 by
Zero to Ten Ltd, part of the Evans Publishing Group
2A Portman Mansions
Chiltern St
London W1U 6NR

First published in Great Britain in 2001 by Zero To Ten Limited, a division
of Evans Publishing Group, 2A Portman Mansions, Chiltern St. London
WlU 6NR

A CIP catalogue record for this book is available from the British Library.

ISBN 1 84089 336 2

Printed in China

SHAPES
ALL AROUND

A FIRST SHAPES BOOK

SALLY SMALLWOOD

Triangles

Triangles have three sides and three pointed corners. Sometimes they point up, sometimes down.

Turn the pages and see how many you can find!

Look
carefully...
triangles can
be hard to spot!

I've got triangles for my breakfast. Have you?

Fold a square of paper in half...

and you make a triangle!

My triangle
is a house
and a roof
and a slide!

I can make triangles with my arms!

Squares

Squares have four sides –
all the same length –
and four corners.

Four squares put together
make one big square.

Turn the pages and see
how many you can find!

Squares can be hard to find.

Here's one now!

And another!
And another!
And another!
And another!

I've found a square...

and I've
made one!

Teddy says "Can you see the squares?"

Look! There are lots of them everywhere!

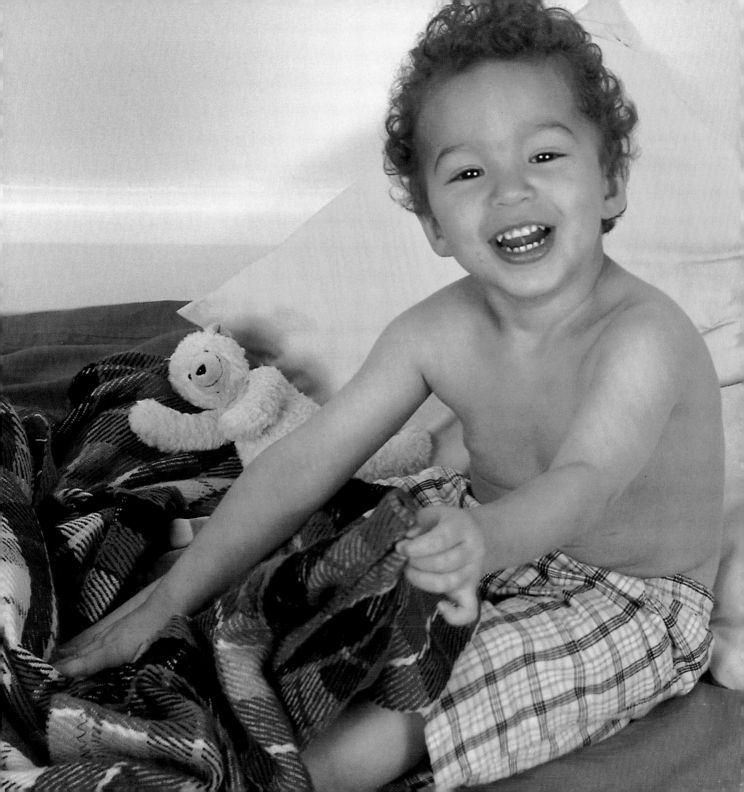

Mum did say she wanted a picture of me...

not quite like this silly!

Circles

Circles have no beginning or end and no corners to hide in. They just go round and round.

Turn the pages and see how many you can find!

You can eat circles for breakfast and wear spots for tea. Spots are circles too!

I'm sure
there's a circle
around here
somewhere...

Watch me paint
some circles.
What colour
are they?

Spits and
spots.
Rain drops!

Rectangles

Rectangles have four sides and four corners. Squares are a kind of rectangle. But these rectangles are different – they have two long sides and two short sides. See how many you can find!

Here's one to wave

...and here's one
to wash with!

Surprises often
come in
rectangles...

I think there's something in here for me!

Here are lots and
lots of them...

I draw on my
rectangles.
Do you?

Shapes are everywhere.
Can you find them?
Can you make some of
your own?